Expressive Writing *1*

A Direct Instruction Program

Workbook

Siegfried Engelmann

Jerry Silbert

Columbus, OH

The **McGraw·Hill** Companies

SRAonline.com

 SRA

2008 Imprint
Copyright © 2005 by SRA/McGraw-Hill.

Send all inquiries to:
SRA/McGraw-Hill
4400 Easton Commons
Columbus, OH 43219

Printed in the United States of America.

ISBN 0-07-603589-1

4 5 6 7 8 9 QPD 11 10 09 08 07

The McGraw·Hill Companies

Lesson 1

Part A

Correct

My class went to the zoo to study seals. We watched the seals for several hours. The zookeeper told us all about seals. She let each of us feed a seal. I fed a seal that was very big. Our class learned a great deal about seals.

Not correct

my class went to the zoo to study seals   we watched the seals for several hours   the zookeeper told us all about seals   she let each of us feed a seal   i fed a seal that was very big   our class learned a great deal about seals

Part B

1. The boy was from New York.   reports   does not report

2. A boy sat on the dock and fished.   reports   does not report

3. The boy wanted to be a boxer.   reports   does not report

4. The girl wore a red swimsuit.   reports   does not report

5. The girl sat in an inner tube.   reports   does not report

6. The girl liked to swim.   reports   does not report

7. The water was very warm.   reports   does not report

8. Several fish fell out of the bucket.   reports   does not report

Part C

1. jump _____ 3. bark _____ 5. spill _____

2. pull _____ 4. push _____ 6. trick _____

Part D

1. _____ ran into the room

2. _____ stood behind his desk

3. _____ made marks on a piece of paper

4. _____ watched the alligator from the front row

Lesson 1   **3**

□ My name

★ Today's date

Part E

1. A dog barked at the car.

2. Her friend was eating lunch in the park.

3. A big bird landed in the barn next to the lake.

□ _____

★ _____

Lesson 2

Part A

Correct

My best friend ran in a ten mile race yesterday morning. People from all over came to run in that race. Six hundred people started the race. Only two hundred people finished the race. My friend came in second. I was very proud of her.

Not correct

my best friend ran in a ten mile race yesterday morning   people from all over came to run in that race   six hundred people started the race   only two hundred people finished the race   my friend came in second   i was very proud of her

Part B

Mrs. Lee

1. Mrs. Lee talked to her sister.   reports   does not report

2. The baby sat on a rug.   reports   does not report

3. The baby had just learned how to walk.   reports   does not report

4. The cat reached toward the bird cage.   reports   does not report

5. The cat was seven years old.   reports   does not report

6. The dog liked to play with the baby.   reports   does not report

7. The baby held on to the dog's tail.   reports   does not report

8. Mrs. Lee was making a birthday cake.   reports   does not report

Part C

1. burn _____   3. push _____   5. start _____

2. fill _____   4. lick _____   6. scratch _____

6   Lesson 2

Part D

1. go	*went*	6. has		11. has	
2. run	*ran*	7. give		12. give	
3. is	*was*	8. run		13. is	
4. has	*had*	9. go		14. run	
5. give	*gave*	10. is		15. go	

Part E

1. _____ put her coat over her head

2. _____ had an umbrella

3. _____ held a newspaper over his head

4. _____ sat on the sidewalk near the woman

Part F

1. A cup fell off the table.
2. Tom and his big sister walked to the park near his house.
3. He read two books last week.
4. The brown horse jumped over a high fence.

Part A

1. Susan, Kathy and Sam held fishing poles.   reports   does not report

2. Susan and Kathy held fishing poles.   reports   does not report

3. Kathy wore shorts.   reports   does not report

4. Kathy held a fishing pole.   reports   does not report

5. Susan and Kathy loved to go fishing.   reports   does not report

6. Sam sat in a boat.   reports   does not report

7. Both girls were wearing shoes.   reports   does not report

8. Susan sat on a blanket that had food on it.   reports   does not report

Part B

The animals were at work. Beavers cut down trees to make dams. Squirrels gathered nuts for the winter. Field mice made little tunnels under the ground. Robins searched for twigs to put in their nests.

the animals were at work   beavers cut down trees to make dams   squirrels gathered nuts for the winter   field mice made little tunnels under the ground robins searched for twigs to put in their nests

Part C

Bill was in the park.

Bill ate an apple.

Bill had two sisters.

Bill wore a new shirt.

Part D

Instructions: Underline the part of each sentence that names.

An old cowboy went to town.

That cowboy rode his horse to town.

He went to town to buy food.

He rode his horse to the food store.

The cowboy went inside.

He bought the food that he needed.

Part E

1. is	*was*	6. go		11. give	
2. go	*went*	7. give		12. has	
3. run	*ran*	8. has		13. run	
4. has	*had*	9. is		14. go	
5. give	*gave*	10. run		15. is	

Part F

Instructions: Complete each sentence so that it tells what happened.

1. The girl _____ running.   (is   was)

2. The horses _____ over the fence.   (jump   jumped)

3. The sun _____ shining.   (was   is)

4. The car _____ at the corner.   (stopped   stops)

5. The dogs _____ their ears.   (scratch   scratched)

Part G

carried two small logs.
petted the dog.
stirred the food in the pot.

1. Mrs. Brown	
2. David	
3. Alex	

Lesson 3   11

Part H

1. Ann and her sister went to the store.
2. My friend had a cold.
3. The class went to the lunchroom.
4. His bike had a flat tire.

Part A

1. Six people worked at the gas station.   reports   does not report

2. Sonya looked under the hood of a car.   reports   does not report

3. Sonya had a flashlight in her back pocket.   reports   does not report

4. Hector held a tire.   reports   does not report

5. Jim and Ray wore hats.   reports   does not report

6. Jim was going home soon.   reports   does not report

Part B

Trina was the tallest student in her class.

Trina played basketball every day.

Trina had long thin arms.

Part C

Instructions: Underline the part of each sentence that names.

A little gray cat looked for its owner. It looked and looked. The poor cat was hungry. The cat made a lot of noise. It went up one street and down another. The cat found its owner. That little cat felt very happy.

Part D

1. has	*had*	6. is	
2. go	*went*	7. give	
3. is	*was*	8. run	
4. give	*gave*	9. go	
5. run	*ran*	10. has	

Part E

Instructions: Complete each sentence so that it tells what happened.

1. They _____ over a log.   (hop   hopped)

2. My big sister _____ fixing her car.   (was   is)

3. He _____ up the book.   (picks   picked)

4. The little bird _____ very thin.   (was   is)

5. I _____ at the cat.   (look   looked)

14   Lesson 4

Part F

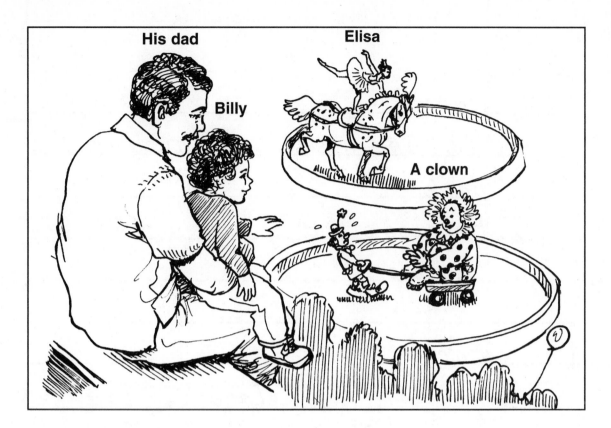

1. _____ sat on his dad's lap

2. _____ put his arm around Billy

3. _____ stood on top of a horse

4. _____ sat in a wagon

Lesson 4   **15**

Part G

1. _Ray and his sister played in the park._

2. _Bernice stood up and walked to the door._

Part H

Ellen helped her dad fix the car. She and her dad worked on the brakes. They fixed the car in three hours.

Part A

1. Matt threw a ball to Lily.	reports	does not report
2. Lily jumped off the ground.	reports	does not report
3. Their mother fell asleep.	reports	does not report
4. The dog stood up on its back legs.	reports	does not report
5. Matt wore a striped swimsuit.	reports	does not report
6. Lily put her hands up.	reports	does not report
7. The teenagers went swimming before they played ball.	reports	does not report
8. Matt and Lily went to the same school.	reports	does not report

Part B

Instructions: Underline the part of each sentence that names.

An old red bike sat in the yard for years. That bike became rusty. It had spider webs on the wheels. A girl decided to fix up the bike. She painted the bike bright red. She put new tires on the bike. The bike looked great. The girl liked the bike.

Part C

1. Ann <u>has</u> two dollars.

2. The mouse <u>runs</u> across the kitchen floor.

3. The runners <u>jump</u> over a log.

4. They <u>go</u> home.

5. The red book <u>is</u> under the chair.

6. Mother robins <u>give</u> worms to their babies.

Part D

Instructions: Fill in the blanks with *he* or *she.*

1. <u>The girl</u> was running.   1. _____ was running.

2. <u>The boy</u> read a book.   2. _____ read a book.

3. <u>Mary</u> painted the wall.   3. _____ painted the wall.

4. <u>Bill</u> walked home.   4. _____ walked home.

5. <u>My brother</u> woke up.   5. _____ woke up.

6. <u>My sister</u> fixed up the car.   6. _____ fixed up the car.

Part E

Instructions: Write sentences that tell what each person did.

| poured | reached | watched | petted | chair | newspaper |

Part F

Bill had a smart dog. The dog could do many tricks. It could walk on its back legs. It could jump through a hoop. All the children liked to play with the smart dog.

Lesson 5   19

Lesson 6

Part A

1. wear	*wore*	6. eat	
2. sit	*sat*	7. bring	
3. throw	*threw*	8. sit	
4. eat	*ate*	9. throw	
5. bring	*brought*	10. wear	

Part B

1. The girls <u>play</u> baseball.

2. My little brother <u>has</u> a cold.

3. The show <u>starts</u> ten minutes late.

4. They <u>go</u> home early.

5. The teacher <u>gives</u> a star to everybody.

6. They <u>run</u> two miles every day.

7. The game <u>is</u> over.

8. Tim <u>has</u> two dollars.

Part C

Instructions: Underline the part of each sentence that names.

A hungry little cat walked into a restaurant. It wanted something to eat. A nice woman owned the restaurant. She gave the cat a bowl of milk. The little animal drank every drop of milk. The woman liked the cat. She made a little bed for it. The cat had a new home.

Part D

Instructions: Fill in the blanks with *he* or *she.*

1. <u>Linda</u> won the race.

1. _____ won the race.

2. <u>Tom</u> went to the park.

2. _____ went to the park.

3. <u>The tall boy</u> washed the car.

3. _____ washed the car.

4. <u>The young woman</u> fixed the bike.

4. _____ fixed the bike.

Part E

tripped	dropped	walked	played
turned	porch	banjo	rocking chair
	ice cream cone		

Lesson 6   21

Part F

    Ann loved to run. She was the fastest runner in her school. She won every race last year. She even beat the teachers.

1 2 3

Check 1: Does each sentence begin with a capital and end with a period?

Check 2: Did you spell all the words correctly?

Check 3: Did you indent the first line and start all the other lines at the margin?

Part A

Instructions: Cross out the sentences that do not report what the picture shows.

A king was counting money. He sat on a big soft chair. He had four stacks of coins on the table. His crown weighed over ten pounds. Each stack of coins was the same size. The king had been working all day. He wore a long robe and a crown.

Part B

Instructions: Underline the part of each sentence that names.

A poor boy found a green wallet on the street. He looked inside. The wallet was very thick. It had enough money in it to buy a house. An old woman came by. She asked the boy if he had seen a green wallet. The boy told her that he had found it. The old woman smiled. She told him that he was a very good boy for telling the truth. She took all the money from the wallet. She gave it to the boy.

Part C

1. wear	*wore*	6. sit	
2. bring	*brought*	7. throw	
3. eat	*ate*	8. wear	
4. sit	*sat*	9. bring	
5. throw	*threw*	10. eat	

Part D

1. They <u>fold</u> the paper in half.

2. The lion <u>has</u> a thorn in its paw.

3. Carlos <u>is</u> taller than Kevin.

4. The girls <u>run</u> as fast as lightning.

5. The men <u>brush</u> their hair.

6. It <u>is</u> sunny outside.

Part E

Instructions: Write a sentence that tells what each person did.

read	petted	watched	leaned	sandwich
newspaper		cell phone	talked	held

Part F

1.

Norma

2.

Yancy

- Norma wore overalls and a scarf.
- Norma put one hand on the board.
- Norma sawed a board.
- Norma put her knee on the board.

- Yancy waved his hand in the air.
- Yancy went up in the air.
- The horse kicked up its back legs.
- Yancy tried to ride the horse.

Part G

	Part G
	Jason had a bad day.
	He missed breakfast because he
	woke up late. He had to walk
	to school in the rain.
	□1 □2 □3

Check 1: Does each sentence begin with a capital and end with a period?

Check 2: Did you spell all the words correctly?

Check 3: Did you indent the first line and start all the other lines at the margin?

Lesson 8

Part A

1. take	*took*	6. buy		11. buy	
2. buy	*bought*	7. fall		12. get	
3. get	*got*	8. are		13. take	
4. are	*were*	9. get		14. are	
5. fall	*fell*	10. take		15. fall	

Part B

Instructions: Fix up the sentences so that they tell what happened.

1. The horses <u>pull</u> the wagon.

2. Tammy <u>is</u> in first place.

3. Alice <u>throws</u> the ball.

4. He <u>has</u> two pencils.

5. They <u>run</u> to the store.

6. We <u>pick</u> flowers.

Part C

Instructions: Underline the part of each sentence that names.

Maria was teaching her horse to do new tricks. She loved to teach tricks to her horse. That horse learned new tricks quickly. It had already learned many tricks. It was able to count by nodding its head. It was able to roll over. The young teacher was proud of her horse. She thought it was the smartest horse she had ever seen.

Part D

1.

Kim

- Kim jumped high into the air.
- Kim was in front of a fence.
- Kim caught a ball.
- Kim reached high over her head.

2.

Jim

- Jim held a can of paint.
- Jim stood on a ladder.
- The wall had paint on it.
- Jim painted a wall.

3.

Tim

- Tim wore a jacket.
- Tim rode a bike.
- Tim held the handlebars.
- Tim could go very fast.

4.

Mr. Garcia

- Mr. Garcia looked at the water.
- Mr. Garcia had a funny hat and high rubber boots.
- The fish tried to get off the line.
- Mr. Garcia caught a large fish on his line.

Part E

Instructions: Write a paragraph that reports on what Robert did. Copy the sentence that tells the main thing Robert did. Then make up at least two more sentences that tell what he did. Begin each new sentence with *He.*

Robert

talked	wrote	telephone	stool	wore
apron	numbers	piece	shoulder	paper
sat	clipboard	bunch	bananas	

	Part E
	Robert worked at the
	store. He
	1 2 3 4

Check 1: Does each sentence begin with a capital and end with a period?
Check 2: Does each sentence tell what the person did?
Check 3: Does each sentence report on what the picture shows?
Check 4: Does each new sentence you made up begin with *He?*

Lesson 9

Part A

1. buy	*bought*	6. buy		11. get	
2. fall	*fell*	7. take		12. are	
3. take	*took*	8. get		13. fall	
4. are	*were*	9. are		14. buy	
5. get	*got*	10. fall		15. take	

Part B

Instructions: Fix up the sentences so that they tell what happened.

1. Our team <u>has</u> seven players.

2. The girl <u>wears</u> a hat.

3. We <u>go</u> to the zoo.

4. Tim <u>sits</u> in the front seat.

5. The train <u>is</u> ten minutes late.

6. We <u>push</u> the heavy door.

7. My friend <u>has</u> a pet snake.

Part C

Instructions: Underline the part of each sentence that names.

A girl bought a dirty old car from her friend. Her dad did not like the car. He told her that the car was in poor shape. She told him that she thought it was a great car. The girl worked on the car every night for two months. She made it look like a brand new car. Her dad even liked it now. The girl gave the car to her dad for his birthday.

Part D

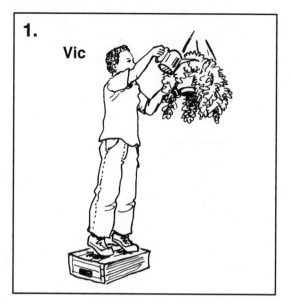

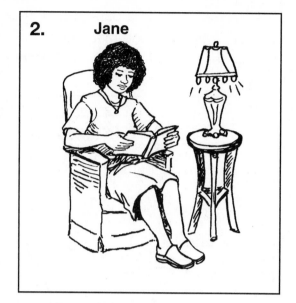

- Vic stood on his tiptoes.
- Vic held the watering can with one hand.
- Vic watered the plant.
- Vic was standing on a box.

- Jane wore a shirt.
- Jane sat by a lamp.
- Jane read a book.
- Jane held something.

Part E

Instructions: Write sentences that tell the main thing each person did.

1. Keisha

2. The astronaut

3. Tanya

| jumped | drank | tied | glass | rock | shoes | laces |

Part F

Instructions: Write a paragraph that reports on what Julia did. Copy the sentence that tells the main thing Julia did. Then make up at least two more sentences that tell what she did. Begin each new sentence with *She.*

Julia

| backwards | air | waved | ice cream cone | sidewalk | smiled |

	Part F
	Julia skated in the park.
	She
	1 2 3 4

Check 1: Does each sentence begin with a capital and end with a period?

Check 2: Does each sentence tell what the person did?

Check 3: Does each sentence report on what the picture shows?

Check 4: Does each new sentence you made up begin with *She?*

Lesson 10

Part A

1. buy	*bought*	6. buy		11. are	
2. fall	*fell*	7. are		12. fall	
3. get	*got*	8. take		13. get	
4. are	*were*	9. fall		14. take	
5. take	*took*	10. get		15. buy	

Part B

Instructions: Fix up the sentences so that they tell what happened.

1. The clown has a big red nose.

2. He is very tired.

3. My mother fixes the car.

4. We go home.

5. I climb up the stairs.

6. Jim has a broken leg.

7. Latrell throws the ball to Jack.

Part C

Instructions: Underline the part of each sentence that names.

The yellow moth began to fly when the sun set. It had large brown spots on each wing. A young hawk also came out. The hawk flew in large circles. It looked for something to eat. The yellow moth flew in crazy little circles. The bird spotted the moth and dove for it. The hawk flew straight at the spot on one wing. The moth flew away with part of its wing missing. The young hawk found something else for dinner.

Part D

Instructions: Write sentences that tell the main thing each person did.

1. Steve	**2. Teresa**	**3. A man**

picture	washed	sawed	painted	board
	bath	cleaned		

Part E

Instructions: Write a paragraph that reports on what Kevin did. Copy the sentence that tells the main thing Kevin did. Then make up at least two more sentences that tell what he did. Begin each new sentence with *He.*

| threw | bicycle | cart | gloves | handlebars | porch | pedaled |

	Part E
	Kevin delivered newspapers.
	He
	1 2 3 4 ☐ ☐ ☐ ☐

Check 1: Does each sentence begin with a capital and end with a period?
Check 2: Does each sentence tell what the person did?
Check 3: Does each sentence report on what the picture shows?
Check 4: Does each new sentence you made up begin with *He?*

Lesson 11

Part A

Instructions: Put in the capitals and periods. Underline the part of each sentence that names.

A young boy threw a ball the ball went over his friend's head it rolled into the street a big truck ran over the ball the truck driver gave the boys a new ball they thanked the truck driver

Part B

Instructions: Change each sentence so that it tells what happened.

1. The books fall off the table.

2. Rodney and Mark fix the broken toy.

3. The key is under the book.

4. Tom has a nail in his shoe.

5. The cat spills the milk.

6. Nick and Roy clean their room.

Part C

Instructions: Fill in each blank with *he, she* or *it.*

1. The car broke down.	1. _____ broke down.
2. The dream went on for an hour.	2. _____ went on for an hour.
3. The young boy sat in a chair.	3. _____ sat in a chair.
4. The monkey was laughing.	4. _____ was laughing.
5. My older sister helped me.	5. _____ helped me.
6. The pen fell off the table.	6. _____ fell off the table.

Part D

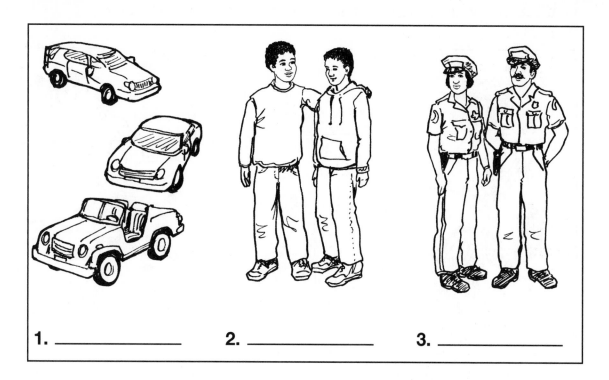

1. _____   2. _____   3. _____

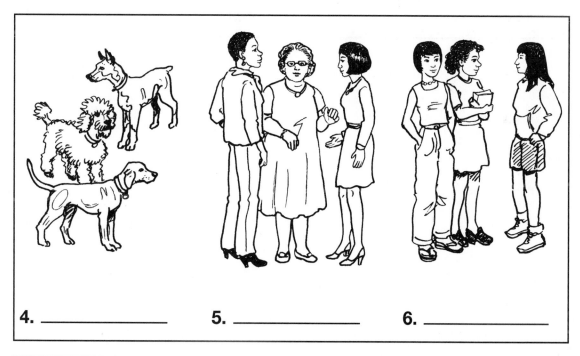

4. _____   5. _____   6. _____

| boys | girls | cars | bikes | women |
| police officers | | dogs | | children |

Lesson 11   **37**

Part E

Instructions: Write sentences that tell the main thing each person did.

1. A woman

2. A boy

3. Yoko

rode	pedaled	pushed	bicycle	high chair
tray	swept	threw	bowl	floor	broom

Part F

Instructions: Write a paragraph that reports on Doris. Begin your paragraph with a sentence that tells the main thing Doris did. Then write at least two more sentences that tell what she did.

| painted | wall | ladder | paintbrush |
| held | | stood | |

Check 1: Does each sentence begin with a capital and end with a period?

Check 2: Does each sentence tell what the person did?

Check 3: Does each sentence report on what the picture shows?

Check 4: Does the first sentence begin with *Doris,* and do the rest of the sentences begin with *She?*

Part A

Instructions: Change each sentence so that it tells what happened.

1. Four people go to the beach.

2. The women play softball.

3. The red bird has a twig in its mouth.

4. Bill is taller than Sam.

5. Rosa pulls the wagon behind her bike.

6. I go fishing in the morning.

Part B

Instructions: Put in the capitals and periods. Underline the part of each sentence that names.

A boat was sinking the passengers jumped off the side of the boat a large whale swam over to the people they climbed onto the whale it took the people back to the shore

Part C

Instructions: Fill in each blank with *he, she* or *it*.

1. The shirt was covered with dirt.   1. _____ was covered with dirt.

2. The rubber ball fell off the table.   2. _____ fell off the table.

3. The boy sat in a chair.   3. _____ sat in a chair.

4. The book was very funny.   4. _____ was very funny.

5. The young woman rode a bike.   5. _____ rode a bike.

6. The game ended at four o'clock.   6. _____ ended at four o'clock.

Part D

1. _____ 2. _____ 3. _____

4. _____ 5. _____ 6. _____

trucks	children	police officers	fire fighters
men	boats	horses	girls	dogs	boys

Lesson 12   41

Part E

Instructions: Write sentences that tell the main thing each person did.

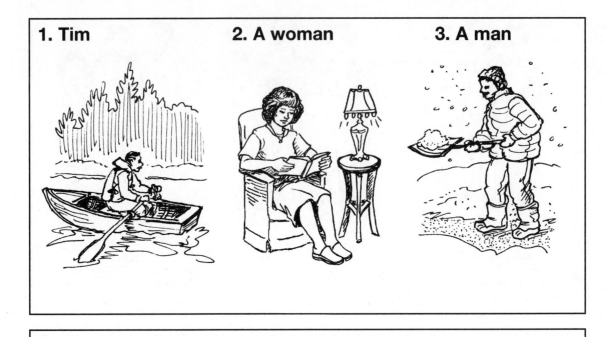

1. Tim **2. A woman** **3. A man**

| read | boat | shoveled | snow | rowed |

Part F

Instructions: Write a paragraph that reports on Mr. James. Begin your paragraph with a sentence that tells the main thing Mr. James did. Then write at least two more sentences that tell what he did.

fed	stool	teddy bear	spoon
	leaned		forward

Check 1: Does each sentence begin with a capital and end with a period?

Check 2: Does each sentence tell what the person did?

Check 3: Does each sentence report on what the picture shows?

Check 4: Does the first sentence begin with *Mr. James,* and do the rest of the sentences begin with *He?*

Lesson 13

Part A

Instructions: Fix up the passage so that all the sentences tell what happened.

A little bird falls out of its nest. The bird is sitting on the cold ground under a tree. Sam and Jane walk past the tree. The bird starts chirping. Sam and Jane go over to the bird. They pick up the bird. They help it get back into its nest.

Part B

Instructions: Put in the capitals and periods. Underline the part of each sentence that names.

His mom covered her eyes she had never seen such a dirty room dirty clothes covered the floor dirty dishes covered the table the room smelled terrible the boy's mom looked angry

Part C

Instructions: Fill in each blank with *he, she* or *it.*

1. My big sister parked the car.   1. _____ parked the car.

2. The red bird sat on a wire.   2. _____ sat on a wire.

3. The little boy painted the fence.   3. _____ painted the fence.

4. The movie was interesting.   4. _____ was interesting.

5. Sally won the race.   5. _____ won the race.

6. The party went on for hours.   6. _____ went on for hours.

Part D

The fire fighters did many brave things.

Fire fighter Jane pulled a man out of a burning car. Fire fighter Bill washed the fire truck. Fire fighter Ron jumped into icy water to save a cat. Police officer Ann stopped two men who tried to rob a bank. Fire fighter Ramon ran into a burning building and carried out a little boy. Fire fighter Jim ate an orange this morning.

Part E

1.
- The children swept the floor.
- A girl cleaned the room.
- The children cleaned the room.
- The children were standing.

2.
- The mechanics wore overalls.
- A man held a tire.
- The woman fixed a car.
- The mechanics worked on vehicles.

3.
- The girls sat in chairs.
- A girl had a ribbon in her hair.
- The girls ate a meal.
- The girls sat around a table.

4.
- The men played basketball.
- The men jumped up.
- The basketball court was made of wood.
- A man shot the basketball.

Part F

Instructions: Write a paragraph that reports on what the king did.

counted	money	coins	stacks	table	stool
robe	crown	slippers	numbers	feather	

Check 1: Does each sentence begin with a capital and end with a period?

Check 2: Does each sentence tell what the person did?

Check 3: Does each sentence report on what the picture shows?

Check 4: Does your paragraph begin with a sentence that tells the main thing the king did?

Part A

Instructions: Fill in the blanks with *he, she* or *it.*

1. Robert spent all morning cleaning his room. _____ put his dirty clothes in the laundry basket. _____ washed the floor and the windows.

2. My sister went to the park. _____ played basketball with her friends for two hours. _____ scored twenty points.

3. The boat went around the small lake. _____ had three sails. _____ moved very quickly across the water.

Part B

Instructions: Fix up each sentence so that it tells what the person did.

1. The boy was eating lunch.

2. The girl was running home.

3. The boy was playing soccer.

4. He was drinking water.

5. She was driving a bus.

drank	drove	ate	played	ran

Part C

Instructions: Put in the capitals and periods. Underline the part of each sentence that names.

Our class played basketball in the gym my team scored twenty points the other team scored thirty points they won the game our teacher told us we did a good job she let us have free time just before school ended

Part D

Our family worked in the yard.

My mom mowed the grass. My dad dug holes for the new trees we were going to plant. My teacher raked the leaves in his yard. My brother read a book about the stars. My sister watered all the flowers in the yard. Two girls washed their bikes.

Part E

1.
- The children stood in a room.
- The girl drew a picture.
- The boy was smiling.
- The children made a mess.

2.
- The animals had eyes.
- A bear rode a bike.
- The animals did tricks.
- The animals wore clothing.

3.
- The cats had long tails.
- The cats played with a ball of string.
- A cat chewed on the string.
- The string was on the floor.

4.
- The woman dug a hole.
- The people were outside.
- The people wore shirts.
- The people worked in the yard.

Part F

Instructions: Write a paragraph that reports on what the clown did.

tightrope	blindfold	striped	across
umbrella	wore	walked	air	held

Check 1: Does each sentence begin with a capital and end with a period?

Check 2: Does each sentence tell what the person did?

Check 3: Does each sentence report on what the picture shows?

Check 4: Does your paragraph begin with a sentence that tells the main thing the clown did?

Test 1

Part A

Instructions: Change each sentence so that it tells what happened.

1. My uncles fix the car.

2. We go to the movies yesterday.

3. The toys fall off the table.

4. My sister and I clean our room.

5. They run to the store.

6. James and Raymond push the car up the hill.

Part B

Instructions: Put in the capitals and periods. Underline the part of each sentence that names.

Albert and Susan made a cherry pie they brought the pie to school the pie was very big their teacher cut the pie into pieces she gave a piece of pie to every student everybody was happy

Part C

Instructions: Fill in the blanks with *he, she* or *it.*

1. His mother was very nice.   1. _____ was very nice.

2. My new bike is great.   2. _____ is great.

3. Tim fixed the bike.   3. _____ fixed the bike.

4. The airplane landed.   4. _____ landed.

Part D

Instructions: Write a paragraph that reports on what Mr. Johnson did.

| stood | roller | wore | used | ladder | overalls |

Check 1: Does each sentence begin with a capital and end with a period?

Check 2: Does each sentence tell what the person did?

Check 3: Does the first sentence begin with *Mr. Johnson,* and do the rest of the sentences begin with *He?*

Check 4: Does your paragraph begin with a sentence that tells the main thing Mr. Johnson did?

Part A

A young boy threw a ball. The ball goes over his friend's head. It rolls into the street. A big truck ran over the ball. The truck driver gives the boys a new ball. They thank the truck driver.

Part B

Instructions: Fill in the blanks with *he, she* or *it.*

1. Linda went to the store. _____ bought an apple. _____ gave the clerk one dollar.

2. Tom brushed his teeth. _____ washed his face. _____ combed his hair.

3. The leaf turned orange. _____ fell off the tree. _____ landed on the ground.

Part C

The men cleaned the room.

James swept the floor. Robert washed the walls. Bill watched a basketball game. Tom wiped the dirt off the windows. Helen washed her clothes. Frank mopped the floors. A little dog barked at a cat.

Part D

Instructions: Fix up each sentence so that it tells what the person or thing did.

1. He was taking a bath.
2. She was looking at the sky.
3. The dog was licking my face.
4. She was building a fire.
5. The teacher was sitting on a chair.
6. She was folding the paper.

| built | folded | licked | looked | sat | took |

Part E

- A man walked in the water.
- A man held a dog.
- The men crossed the river.
- A man walked on a log.

- The girls jumped up.
- The girls reached up.
- A girl tried to catch a football.
- The girls tried to catch the balls.

- The clowns entertained the children.
- A clown stood on his hands.
- The clowns wore costumes.
- A clown walked across a tightrope.

- The women held tools.
- A woman hammered nails into a beam.
- The women were building a house.
- The women wore work clothes.

54   Lesson 16

Part F

Instructions: Copy the title sentence. Then write a paragraph that reports on the picture. Start your paragraph with a sentence that tells the main thing person 1 did. Then write a sentence that tells the main thing person 2 did. Then write a sentence that tells the main thing person 3 did.

The family went camping.

stirred	carried	cooked	logs	spoon
roasted		stick		pile

Check 1: Does each sentence begin with a capital and end with a period?

Check 2: Does each sentence tell what a person did?

Check 3: Does each sentence report on the main thing a person did?

Lesson 17

Part A

Tamika helped Tim do his homework. Tim has three pages of math problems. Tamika shows Tim how to do several problems. Tim did the rest of the problems by himself. Tim works for three hours. Tim and Tamika go out for pizza when he finished his homework.

Part B

Instructions: Fill in the blanks with *he, she* or *it.*

1. His sister liked to run. _____ ran five miles every morning before breakfast.
2. The toy car didn't work. _____ needed new batteries.
3. My brother stayed home yesterday. _____ had a cold.
4. The plate fell off the table. _____ broke into many pieces when it hit the floor.

Part C

Instructions: Underline the part of each sentence that names.

Bill's sister told Bill that she would take him for a ride in her airplane. Bill had never been in a plane before. He felt frightened. His sister told him not to worry. They got into the plane. His sister started the motor. The plane took off. Bill looked out the window. The ground looked very pretty from the plane. Bill enjoyed his first plane ride.

Part D

Instructions: Fix up each sentence so that it tells what the persons did.

1. They were wearing helmets.
2. She was throwing the ball.
3. They were cleaning the room.
4. The boys were sitting on the floor.
5. He was wearing a new shirt.
6. The clown was rubbing his nose.

| sat | threw | rubbed | wore | cleaned |

Part E

Instructions: Write a good title sentence for each picture.

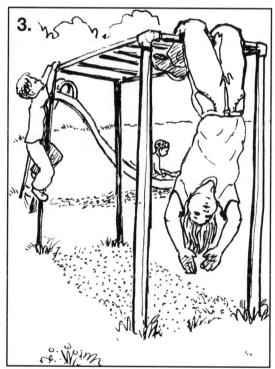

<u>the boys</u>	<u>the children</u>	<u>the dogs</u>	<u>the people</u>	picked	carried
pulled	played	house	chair	apples	park	sled	snow

Lesson 17   **57**

Part F

Instructions: Copy the title sentence. Then write a paragraph that reports on the picture. Start your paragraph with a sentence that tells the main thing person 1 did. Then write a sentence that tells the main thing person 2 did. Then write a sentence that tells the main thing person 3 did.

The police officers ate breakfast.

1. Officer James **2. Officer Bob** **3. Officer Ann**

| police officer | breakfast | jelly | bread | spread |
| toast | cut | pancakes | syrup | poured | cereal | piece |

Check 1: Does each sentence begin with a capital and end with a period?

Check 2: Does each sentence tell what a person did?

Check 3: Does each sentence report on the main thing a person did?

Lesson 18

Part A

The ants searched for food. A little ant found a huge strawberry. That ant calls the other ants. They marched over to the strawberry. The ants carried the strawberry back to their ant hill. They chew the strawberry into smaller pieces. They carried the small pieces into the ant hill. The ants have a big meal that night.

Part B

Instructions: Fix up each sentence so that it tells what the persons did.

1. She was riding a horse.

2. The girls were talking loudly.

3. The men were painting the room.

4. He was holding the baby.

5. She was standing on a chair.

6. They were washing the windows.

held	painted	rode	stood	talked	washed

Part C

Instructions: Cross out some of the names and write *he, she* or *it*.

Ⓐ Mario found many things when he went walking. Ⓑ Mario once found a striped cat. Ⓒ That cat was very thin. Ⓓ That cat was sitting on the sidewalk. Ⓔ Mario took the cat home with him. Ⓕ Mario tried to hide the cat from his mother. Ⓖ His mother heard the cat. Ⓗ His mother liked the cat and told Mario that he could keep it.

Part D

the painters	the cooks	the girls	the children
painted played	cleaned	baseball meal	food house
	prepared	wall room	

60   Lesson 18

Part E

Instructions: Write a good title sentence. Then write a paragraph that reports on the picture.

children	swept	washed	cleaned	room	floor
	window		wall		marks

Check 1: Does each sentence begin with a capital and end with a period?
Check 2: Does each sentence tell what a person did?
Check 3: Does each sentence report on the main thing a person did?

Lesson 19

Part A

Instructions: Put in the capitals and periods. Underline the part of each sentence that names.

the women fixed up an old car they made the car look brand new mary put a new engine into the car she also fixed the brakes mary's sister painted the outside of the car they sold the fixed-up car for nine hundred dollars they used the money to buy a new motorcycle

Part B

Instructions: Cross out some of the names and write *he, she* or *it.*

Ⓐ Tom wanted to cook a meatloaf. Ⓑ Tom got a cookbook from his mom. Ⓒ The cookbook told how to make many things. Ⓓ The cookbook told how to fix eggs, chicken and meatloaf. Ⓔ Tom found the page that told about fixing meatloaf. Ⓕ Tom followed the directions for making meatloaf. Ⓖ His mom ate the meatloaf. Ⓗ His mom told Tom that it was very good.

Part C

Instructions: Rewrite each sentence so that it tells what the person or thing did.

1. The boy was chasing a dog.

2. The girl was washing the car.

3. He was writing a letter.

4. She was eating apples.

5. The airplane was taking off.

| took | chased | wrote | ate | washed |

Part D

Instructions: Each person wore something that is unusual. Write a sentence that tells about the unusual thing each person wore.

1. A woman   **2. A lifeguard**   **3. The actor**

dress	helmet	pants	mittens	suit
swim fins		flippers		pair

Lesson 19   **63**

Part E

Instructions: Write a good title sentence. Then write a paragraph that reports on the picture.

cooks	meal	food	tomato	sliced	salad	prepared	grill
oven	cooked	kitchen	loaf	bread	baked	worked	took

Check 1: Does each sentence begin with a capital and end with a period?

Check 2: Does each sentence tell what a person did?

Check 3: Does each sentence report on the main thing a person did?

Lesson 20

Part A

Instructions: Underline the part of each sentence that names.

The weather got very cold last night. A pipe broke in our classroom. Water poured out of the pipe all night long. The floor was under three feet of water by the morning. The water turned to ice. The teacher almost fell over when he opened the door. His room looked like it had turned into an ice-skating rink.

Part B

Instructions: Cross out some of the names and write *he, she* or *it.*

Ⓐ Trina loved to look for things on the sidewalk. Ⓑ Trina found three bugs, two rocks and a baseball yesterday. Ⓒ Her father did not like some of the things she found. Ⓓ Her father did not like the bugs that Trina brought home. Ⓔ Trina's brother liked one of the things Trina found. Ⓕ Trina's brother liked the baseball.

Part C

Instructions: Rewrite each sentence so that it tells what the persons did.

1. The men were telling jokes.

2. She was picking up the pencils.

3. They were washing the car.

4. He was sitting on a log.

5. She was painting the wall.

| painted | told | sat | washed | picked |

Part D

Instructions: Write two sentences that report on each person. The first sentence should tell the main thing the person did. The second sentence should tell about the unusual thing the person wore.

1. A young woman

2. Arthur

chopped	shoveled	wore	bathing suit
business suit	ax	boots	tie snow

Part E

Instructions: Write a good title sentence. Then write a paragraph that reports on the picture.

1. The boss

2. A carpenter

3. Their helper

women	hammered	worked on	board	nailed
sawed	carried	building	house	were

Check 1: Does each sentence begin with a capital and end with a period?

Check 2: Does each sentence tell what a person did?

Check 3: Does each sentence report on the main thing a person did?

Lesson 21

Part A

Instructions: If a word is somebody's name, begin the word with a capital letter.

nancy   he   truck   tammy   james   they

andrew   ann   jack   my   sam   helen   she

window   tim   it

Part B

Instructions: Cross out some of the names and write *he, she* or *it.*

James had a birthday yesterday. James was eleven years old. His mother brought a big birthday cake to school. His mother gave a piece of cake to each person in James' class. The cake tasted great. The cake had chocolate icing.

Part C

Instructions: Rewrite each sentence so that it tells what the person or persons did.

1. The girls were running up the hill.
2. My mother was helping me fix my bike.
3. The boys were taking turns.
4. His sister was driving the car.
5. The men were talking about the game.

talked	went	drove	took	helped	ran

Part D

Instructions: Write two sentences that report on each person. The first sentence should tell the main thing the person did. The second sentence should tell about the unusual thing the person wore.

1. A girl

2. Ramon

jumped	hurdle	juggled	pants
bowling pins		blindfold	skates

Lesson 21   **69**

Part E

Instructions: Write a good title sentence. Then write a paragraph that reports on the picture.

| gas station attendants | | washed | poured | air | window |
| tire | cleaned | garage | worked | station | |

Check 1: Does each sentence begin with a capital and end with a period?

Check 2: Does each sentence tell what a person did?

Check 3: Does each sentence report on the main thing a person did?

Lesson 22

Part A

Instructions: Cross out some of the names and write *he, she* or *it*.

The children watched the circus parade. Kevin jumped up when the lions went by. Kevin had never seen such big animals. His sister took pictures of the animals. His sister used up two rolls of film. The parade lasted two hours. The parade ended just after eight o'clock.

Part B

Instructions: If the words are somebody's name, begin each word with a capital letter.

lamar jenkins   mrs. williams   the doctor   his brother

tyrell washington   jerry martinez   this boy   mr. adams

the girl   the nurse   mrs. cash

Part C

Instructions: Underline the part of each sentence that names.

The big storm lasted two hours. The wind knocked over several trees. A big tree fell into the middle of the street. It blocked traffic. A bulldozer had to push the tree off the street. Everybody stayed inside until the storm had ended.

Part D

Instructions: Rewrite the sentences to tell what the persons or things did.

1. She was talking on the phone.
2. The dogs were barking loudly.
3. She was holding the cat.
4. The women were working very hard.
5. The children were sitting on little chairs.

| held | sat | worked | talked | barked |

Part E

Instructions: Write a good title sentence. Then write a paragraph that reports on the picture. Write two sentences about each person. The first sentence about a person should tell the main thing the person did. The second sentence should tell what the person wore.

children	beach	played	dug	built	pushed

sand	sand castle	beach ball	overalls

swimsuit	diaper

Check 1: Does each sentence begin with a capital and end with a period?

Check 2: Does your first sentence about each person report on the main thing the person did?

Check 3: Does your second sentence about each person begin with *he* or *she*?

Check 4: Does each sentence tell what a person did?

Lesson 23

Part A

Instructions: Fix up the passage so that all the sentences tell what the person did, not what the person was doing.

Marcus woke up late. He was running down the stairs. He grabbed his school book. He was jumping onto his bike. He rode the bike as fast as he could. He was parking the bike. He ran into the classroom. He was sitting in his chair.

Part B

Instructions: If the words are somebody's name, begin each word with a capital letter.

alan davis   mrs. robinson   the nurse   her sister

manuel ortíz   a police officer   my teacher   a tiger

mr. james   helen smith   a clown   vanessa martin

Part C

Instructions: Make up sentences that tell what the people had. Make sure that each sentence tells only about one person, not about more than one person.

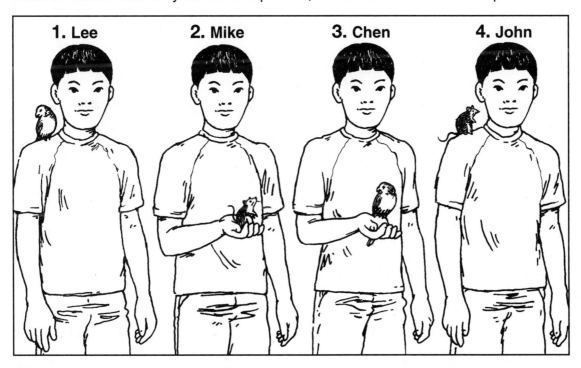

| parrot | mouse | shoulder | hand |

Part D

Instructions: Rewrite the sentences to tell what the persons did.

1. They were eating lunch.

2. My sister was pushing me.

3. He was sitting on the floor.

4. The women were fixing the car.

5. The children were talking quietly.

fixed	talked	pushed	ate	sat

Part E

Instructions: Write a good title sentence. Then write a paragraph that reports on the picture. Write two sentences about each dog. The first sentence about each dog should tell the main thing the dog did. The second sentence should tell what the dog wore.

1. A boxer   2. A poodle   3. A collie

tricks	stood	jumped	balanced	back	hoop
nose	collar	hat	sunglasses		through

Check 1: Does each sentence begin with a capital and end with a period?

Check 2: Does your first sentence about each dog report on the main thing the dog did?

Check 3: Does your second sentence about each dog begin with *it*?

Check 4: Does each sentence tell what an animal did?

Lesson 24

Part A

Instructions: Cross out some of the names and write *he, she* or *it.*

Jack looked for his dog. Jack wanted to give the dog a bath. The dog did not like baths. The dog hid behind a bush. Jack asked his sister to help him find the dog. They looked for an hour, but they couldn't find the dog. His sister had an idea. His sister threw a ball into the air. The dog loved to play. The dog jumped out from behind the bush. The children saw the dog. The dog caught the ball. The children caught the dog.

Part B

Instructions: If the words are somebody's name, begin the words with capital letters.

greg carter   mrs. alvarez   my sister   a cowboy   ronnie lee

a poodle   jerry adams   mr. sanders   this cat

the fire fighter   peggy   mrs. jackson

Part C

Instructions: Fix up the passage so that all the sentences tell what the person did, not what the person was doing.

Jerry heard a noise. He was seeing a little kitten on the sidewalk. He picked up the kitten. He was taking it home with him. He was giving it some water. He made a little bed for it. He loved his new pet.

Lesson 24   **75**

Part D

Instructions: Make up sentences that tell what each man had. Make sure that each sentence tells only about one person, not about more than one person.

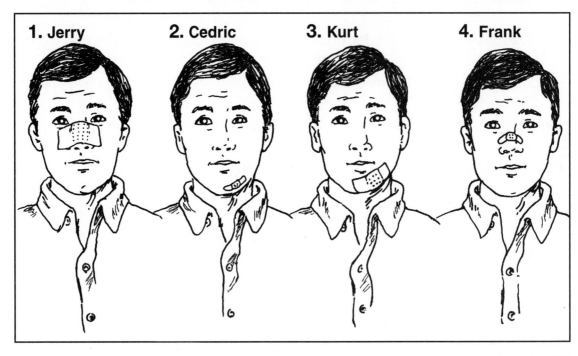

| 1. Jerry | 2. Cedric | 3. Kurt | 4. Frank |

| bandage | little | nose | chin |

Part E

Instructions: Rewrite each sentence so that it tells what the person or persons did.

1. She was putting candles on the cake.

2. They were sitting on the floor.

3. Jerry was picking up his clothes.

4. They were washing the walls.

5. Susan was holding a glass.

| picked | put | sat | held | washed |

Part F

Instructions: Write a good title sentence. Then write a paragraph that reports on the picture. Write two sentences about each clown. The first sentence about each clown should tell the main thing the clown did. The second sentence should tell what the clown had.

1. Jessica

2. Travis

clowns	entertained	children	stood	walked
parrot	tightrope	monkey	shoulder	

Check 1: Does each sentence begin with a capital and end with a period?

Check 2: Does your first sentence about each clown report on the main thing the clown did?

Check 3: Does your second sentence about each clown begin with *he* or *she*?

Check 4: Does each sentence tell what a person did?

Lesson 24   77

Lesson 25

Part A

Instructions: Fix up the passage so that each part of somebody's name begins with a capital.

Herman was a big fish. He did not like fishermen. ralph jackson was a fisherman. Herman did not like mr. Jackson. Mr. jackson went fishing one day at the pond where herman lived. Herman saw the hook at the end of mr. Jackson's line. He pulled on the line so hard that mr. jackson fell into the water. herman laughed as he watched the fisherman get into his boat. Mr. Jackson never went back to the pond where herman lived.

Part B

Tom threw a snowball at his friend. And it hit his friend's leg. And then his friend chased him. And they both ran as fast as they could. His friend caught Tom in the middle of the park. And then Tom told his friend that he was sorry for hitting him in the leg with the snowball. The boys shook hands. And they were still friends.

Part C

Instructions: Fix up the passage so that all the sentences tell what the person did, not what the person was doing.

Shameka bought a little tree. She was digging a hole in her yard. She put the tree into the hole. She was filling the hole with dirt. She was watering the tree. She built a little fence around the tree.

Part D

Instructions: Rewrite the sentences to tell what the persons did.

1. The clown was doing tricks.

2. Anita was giving her dog a bath.

3. The men were making breakfast.

4. The little girl was messing up the room.

5. The women were planting trees.

made	did	gave	planted	messed

Part E

Instructions: Copy the good title sentence. Then write a paragraph that reports on what Ben did.

> Ben washed the wall.
>
> Ben wore pants and a shirt.
>
> Ben cleaned the room.

made	picked	clothes	washed
drawings	marks	wall	cleaned

Check 1: Does each sentence begin with a capital and end with a period?

Check 2: Does each sentence tell what Ben did, not what Ben was doing?

Check 3: Does the first sentence begin with *Ben,* and do the rest of the sentences begin with *he?*

Lesson 25 79

Part A

Instructions: Fix up the passage so that each part of a person's name begins with a capital.

nancy wilson and jasmine robinson lived in a big city. They wanted to visit their friend who lived on a farm. The girls worked every day after school to earn money for the trip. nancy helped mr. jackson fix his car. jasmine helped mr. baker paint his apartment. nancy and jasmine soon had enough money for the trip.

Part B

A bull chased Pam through a field. Pam jumped over a fence. And then the bull jumped over the fence. And Pam kept on running. And the bull was right behind her. Pam ran over to a tree. And then she climbed up the tree as fast as she could. And the bull waited under the tree until the sun went down. And then Pam climbed down after the bull left. And she knew she shouldn't have taken a shortcut across that field.

Part C

Instructions: Underline the part of each sentence that names.

Richard had the biggest cat in the neighborhood. The cat followed Richard to the school bus stop one morning. It tried to get on the bus. The bus door was too small. Richard's cat got stuck. The kids had to push for an hour to get Richard's cat off the bus.

Part D

Instructions: Copy the good title sentence. Then write a paragraph that reports on what Ana did.

Ana did well in school.

Ana had nice clothes.

Ana had a good day.

found	dollars	race	won
first place	received	ribbon	

Check 1: Does each sentence begin with a capital and end with a period?

Check 2: Does each sentence tell what Ana did, not what Ana was doing?

Check 3: Does the first sentence begin with *Ana,* and do the rest of the sentences begin with *she?*

Lesson 26   81

Part E

Instructions: Copy the good title sentence. Then write a paragraph that reports on what Susan did.

> Susan carried the cat down the ladder.
>
> Susan rescued the cat.
>
> Susan stood near a tree.

| grabbed | carried | climbed | ladder |

Check 1: Does each sentence begin with a capital and end with a period?

Check 2: Does each sentence tell what Susan did, not what Susan was doing?

Check 3: Does the first sentence begin with *Susan,* and do the rest of the sentences begin with *she?*

Lesson 27

Part A

Instructions: Fill in the blank next to each sentence with *he, she, it* or *they*.

1. The man and the woman ate lunch.
1. _____ ate lunch.

2. Lenora and Kedrick walked on the sand.
2. _____ walked on the sand.

3. The truck had a flat tire.
3. _____ had a flat tire.

4. The apples cost 84 cents.
4. _____ cost 84 cents.

5. The women wore red shirts.
5. _____ wore red shirts.

6. The old book was worth a lot of money.
6. _____ was worth a lot of money.

7. Alberto and his dog went jogging.
7. _____ went jogging.

8. The old man wore a long blue coat.
8. _____ wore a long blue coat.

Part B

Instructions: Fix up the passage so that no sentence begins with *and* or *and then*.

Richard had a good day. Richard's teacher gave Richard his report card just before the school day ended. And Richard jumped with joy when he saw the good marks on his report card. And then he ran home to show his mother the report card. And then he gave her the report card. And then his mother read the report card for several minutes. And she was so happy that she made Richard and the rest of the family a big pizza for dinner.

Part C

Janet earned lots of money.

Janet needed money for a new baseball bat. She asked her dad how she could earn some money. Her dad told her the garage needed to be cleaned. Janet cleaned out the garage. Janet liked to swim. Janet's dad gave her five dollars. Janet asked her dad what else she could do. Her dad told Janet that she could sell the junk from the garage. Janet's dad loved to fly airplanes. Janet loaded all the junk from the garage in a wagon. She took the junk to a store that buys old junk. Her sister went to the movies. The man at the junk store told Janet that an old picture in the junk pile was not junk. It was worth three thousand dollars. Janet earned a lot of money that day.

Part D

Instructions: Write a good title sentence. Then write a paragraph that reports on what Jerry did.

tub	bathroom	water	dragged	lifted
brush	gave	filled	washed	

Check 1: Does each sentence begin with a capital and end with a period?

Check 2: Does each sentence tell what Jerry did, not what he was doing?

Check 3: Does the first sentence begin with *Jerry,* and do the rest of the sentences begin with *he?*

84   Lesson 27

Part E

Instructions: Write a good title sentence. Then write a paragraph that reports on the picture. Write two sentences about each person. The first sentence about each person should tell the main thing the person did. The second sentence should tell something else the person did.

2. Gwen

1. Tina

room	ceiling	women	painted	trim
bottom	roller	kneeled	knees	
brushed	used			

Check 1: Does each sentence begin with a capital and end with a period?

Check 2: Does each sentence tell what the person did, not what the person was doing?

Check 3: Does your second sentence about each person begin with *she?*

Part A

Amber and Sam went shopping.

Amber had a pet monkey named Sam. One day Amber took Sam shopping with her at the supermarket. Amber got a grocery cart. She put Sam into the cart. The other people in the store looked at Amber and the monkey. Amber had two pet birds at home. She put many things into the cart. Sam tried to push some of these things out of the cart. Amber scolded the monkey. She lived in a large house with a big backyard. She left Sam sitting in the cart while she went to look for bread. She heard people laughing when she was walking back to her grocery cart. Amber liked to walk in the park every afternoon. She knew why people were laughing when she looked at the cart. All the groceries were on the floor. The cart was filled with bananas.

Part B

Instructions: Fix up the run-on sentences.

1. The boys were playing basketball and their sister walked toward them and they asked her if she wanted to play basketball.

2. A girl ran over to the zookeeper and he turned around and she asked if she could help feed the animals and the zookeeper gave her some peanuts to throw to the elephants.

3. A boy wrote an interesting story and his teacher read it to the class and the children liked the story.

Part C

Instructions: Fill in the blank next to each sentence with *he, she, it* or *they*.

1. A cat and a dog made a mess.

2. The girls went to school.

3. My mother was very pretty.

4. Tyrell and his brother were not home.

5. Four ducks were on the lake.

6. The tables were old.

7. My brother came home late.

8. That car was bright red.

1. _____ made a mess.

2. _____ went to school.

3. _____ was very pretty.

4. _____ were not home.

5. _____ were on the lake.

6. _____ were old.

7. _____ came home late.

8. _____ was bright red.

Part D

Instructions: Write a good title sentence. Then write a paragraph that reports on what the woman did.

planted	dug	filled	tree	hole
dirt	ground	shovel	covered	

Check 1: Does each sentence begin with a capital and end with a period?

Check 2: Does each sentence tell what the woman did, not what the woman was doing?

Check 3: Does the first sentence begin with *the woman,* and do the rest of the sentences begin with *she?*

Part E

Instructions: Write a good title sentence. Then write a paragraph that reports on the picture. Write two sentences about each person. The first sentence about each person should tell the main thing the person did. The second sentence should tell something else the person did.

1. Bill Adams

2. Jerry Lee

men	crossed	stream	walked	log
above	held	carried	water	
clothes	over	head	through	

Check 1: Does each sentence begin with a capital and end with a period?

Check 2: Does each sentence tell what the person did, not what the person was doing?

Check 3: Does your second sentence about each person begin with *he?*

Lesson 29

Part A

Instructions: Edit the passage for these checks:

Check 1: Do any sentences begin with *and* or *and then?*
Check 2: Do all the words that are part of a person's name begin with a capital?

Jasmine and barry found a little bird that had fallen out of its nest. And then they took the little bird home with them. mr. robinson gave them a book about birds. And the book told how to take care of the bird. jasmine fed the bird while barry made a bed for it. And then the bird got better. jasmine and barry took it back to its nest.

Part B

Instructions: Fill in the blank next to each sentence with *he, she, it* or *they.*

1. Tony and his brother went home.
2. A book and a pencil were on the desk.
3. The toy cost less than a dollar.
4. The woman walked past our house.
5. Shawn and Edna ate lunch.
6. A car moved slowly up the hill.
7. The books were on the floor.
8. Six ducks walked across the road.

1. _____ went home.
2. _____ were on the desk.
3. _____ cost less than a dollar.
4. _____ walked past our house.
5. _____ ate lunch.
6. _____ moved slowly up the hill.
7. _____ were on the floor.
8. _____ walked across the road.

Part C

Instructions: Fix up the run-on sentences.

1. Ana hit the ball very hard and the ball went over the fence and the kids cheered for Ana.

2. A man got out of his car and it had a flat tire and the man was not very happy.

3. Ramon watched the boats sail up the river and his favorite boat went by at about three o'clock and it had two big blue sails.

Part D

Instructions: Write sentences that tell what each object did.

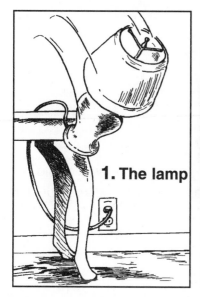

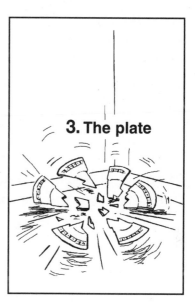

table	backfired	floor	fell	pieces
off	many	broke	shattered	

Lesson 29 **91**

Part E

Instructions: Write a good title sentence. Then write a paragraph that reports on what the man did.

| breakfast | cooked | eggs | piece | bread |
| spread | poured | cereal | bowl | toast |

Check 1: Does each sentence begin with a capital and end with a period?

Check 2: Does each sentence tell what the man did, not what he was doing?

Check 3: Does the first sentence begin with *the man,* and do the rest of the sentences begin with *he?*

Test 2

Part A

Instructions: Fix up the passage so that all the sentences tell what a person did, not what the person was doing.

Jerry looked for his dog. He found the dog hiding under a chair. Jerry was lifting up the dog. He was carrying the dog to the bathtub. He was filling the bathtub with water. He poured soap into the water. He was washing the unhappy dog with a brush.

Part B

Instructions: Put in the capitals and periods. Underline the part of each sentence that names.

Albert and Susan made a big cherry pie they brought the pie to school the pie was big enough to feed thirty children their teacher let them give pieces of pie to all their friends everybody was happy.

Part C

Instructions: Cross out some of the names and write *he, she* or *it.*

Tom's birthday was yesterday. His sister wanted to surprise him. His sister baked something for his birthday. The cake had strawberry icing. The cake was very big. Tom cut the cake into pieces. Tom gave a piece to each of his brothers and sisters.

Part D

Instructions: If the words are somebody's name, begin each word with a capital letter.

mr. johnson   my teacher   her friend   jerry smith   the police officer

michael jones   mrs. robinson   a cowboy   my sister

Part E

Instructions: Write a good title sentence. Then write a paragraph that reports on what Alicia did.

| hamburgers | grilled | bun | cooked | children |

Check 1: Does each sentence begin with a capital and end with a period?

Check 2: Does each sentence tell what Alicia did, not what Alicia was doing?

Check 3: Does the first sentence begin with *Alicia,* and do the rest of the sentences begin with *she?*

Lesson 31

Part A

Instructions: Fix up the run-on sentences.

1. A boy and a girl found a snake and it had black and red stripes and the children showed the snake to their mother and father.

2. John and his sister went to the movies last night and the movie lasted two and a half hours and they went out for pizza and ice cream after the movie.

3. A girl bought an old bike from a friend and the bike had rust on its handlebars and wheels and the girl and her friend fixed up the bike.

Part B

Instructions: Fix up the passage so that all the sentences tell what a person or thing did, not what a person or thing was doing.

A space monster walked toward the boys. They started to run. One boy was falling down. The other boy kept on running. The space monster was looking at the boy who had fallen down. The boy started to cry. The space monster snapped its fingers. An ice cream cone appeared in its hand. The space monster was giving the ice cream cone to the boy.

Part C

3. The younger boy

1. A space creature

2. The older boy

4. The space creature

5. The boys

A space creature waved at two boys who were picking apples. The older boy ran away. The younger boy fell off a branch. The space creature caught the younger boy. The boys gave the space creature a basket filled with apples.

Part D

Instructions: Write a paragraph that reports on what happened.

1. The cowboy

2. The bull

3. A clown

4. The bull   5. The clown

| fell | ground | charged | ran | toward | barrel |
| front | knocked | air | helped | walk | away |

Check 1: Does each sentence begin with a capital and end with a period?

Check 2: Does each sentence tell what a person or thing did, not what a person or thing was doing?

Check 3: Does each sentence report on the main thing a person or thing did in the picture?

Lesson 31   **97**

Part A

Instructions: Fix up the run-on sentences in this passage.

A girl got a big dog for her birthday and the dog was so big that it could not fit through the doors of the girl's house. It had to live outside in a house with big doors. The dog followed the girl to the school bus stop one morning and the girl didn't see the dog behind her and the dog tried to sneak onto the bus. The door of the bus was too small. The dog got stuck and all the children had to push together to get the dog off the bus.

Part B

Instructions: Cross out some of the names and write *he, she, it* or *they.*

Nancy and Paul took turns throwing rocks into the river. Nancy and Paul tried to hit a log that was lying in the middle of the river. Paul threw first. Paul threw the rock too far. It missed the log by ten feet. Nancy threw next. Nancy aimed carefully. The rock hit the log. Something strange happened. The log started to move. The log was really an alligator. The children ran home. The children never played at that river again.

Part C

Instructions: Write sentences that tell what each object did.

| | 1. The bottle | | 2. The ball | | 3. The balloon |

| wastebasket | fence | ceiling | floated | over | fell |
| flew | went | air | toward | | |

Lesson 32   **99**

Part D

Instructions: Write a paragraph that reports on what happened. Write sentences that tell the main thing each numbered thing did.

1. A bluebird

2. A striped cat

3. The cat

4. The bird

5. The branch

6. The cat

| ground | climbed | flew | broke | trunk | branch |

Check 1: Does each sentence begin with a capital and end with a period?

Check 2: Does each sentence tell what something did, not what something was doing?

Check 3: Does each sentence report on the main thing that something did in the picture?

Lesson 33

Part A

Instructions: Cross out some of the names and write *he, she, it* or *they.*

My friends loved to read books. My friends read all kinds of books. Jill had just finished a book about dinosaurs. Jill could name 20 different dinosaurs. Tom liked books about space. Tom had just finished a book about the stars. The book belonged to his uncle. The book had 999 pages.

Part B

Instructions: Fix up the run-on sentences in this passage.

A loud noise woke up a little boy and he ran into his parents' room and his parents were sleeping. The boy woke up his parents. He told them that he had heard a loud noise outside. His mom and dad looked outside. They didn't see anything and his dad told the boy to go back to sleep and the boy went back to his room. He looked out the window. He saw a small spaceship take off.

Part C

Instructions: Put in the capitals and periods.

a woman went to the zoo she watched the monkeys do tricks a big monkey stood on its head the woman took a picture of the big monkey she showed the picture to her grandchildren they liked the picture

Part D

Instructions: Write a sentence that tells what each object did.

| dripped | rolled | hit | tree | side | sink |

Part E

Instructions: Copy the good title sentence. Then write a paragraph that reports on what happened. Write sentences that tell the main thing each numbered person did.

> The children ran.
> Maria ran over the goal line.
> The children played football.

| football | threw | jumped | her brother's leg | dove |
| goal line | caught | tackled | grabbed | sister |

Check 1: Does each sentence begin with a capital and end with a period?

Check 2: Does each sentence tell what the person did, not what the person was doing?

Check 3: Does each sentence report on the main thing the person did in the picture?

Lesson 34

Part A

Instructions: Put in the capitals and periods.

a boy threw a rock at a tree the rock hit a beehive the beehive fell to the ground the bees flew out of the beehive they chased the boy he ran toward a pond he jumped into the pond before the bees reached him

Part B

Instructions: Fix up the run-on sentences in this passage.

A boy and a girl went to the museum with their class and the teacher told the children to be very careful and the boy and the girl did not listen. They went to the dinosaur room and the girl picked up a dinosaur egg. She told the boy that she didn't believe the egg was a real dinosaur egg. He asked the girl to show him the egg. The girl dropped the egg as she started to give it to the boy. The egg broke when it hit the floor and a dinosaur crawled out of the broken egg and the children ran out the door to get their teacher. The dinosaur ran around the room. It knocked over many things. Then it jumped out an open window. Nobody believed the boy and the girl when they told what happened.

Part C

Instructions: Write a good title sentence. Then write a paragraph that reports on what the girl did.

messed	room	made	marks	wall	pulled
table	CDs	threw	papers	book	floor
	wrote	pictures	tore		

Check 1: Does each sentence begin with a capital and end with a period?

Check 2: Does each sentence tell what the girl did, not what the girl was doing?

Check 3: Does the first sentence begin with *the girl,* and do the rest of the sentences begin with *she?*

Part D

Instructions: Write a good title sentence. Then write a paragraph that reports on what happened. Write sentences that tell the main thing each numbered person or thing did.

1. A little bird

2. James

3. His sister

4. James

5. She

bird	helped	fell	its nest	ground	climbed
tree		branch		rescued	

Check 1: Does each sentence begin with a capital and end with a period?

Check 2: Does each sentence tell what a person or thing did, not what a person or thing was doing?

Check 3: Does each sentence report on the main thing a person or thing did in the picture?

Lesson 35

Part A

1. Tyrell stood up and waved to his friend.

2. A girl jumped up and clapped her hands.

3. My friend stopped walking and waited for the light to turn green.

Part B

Instructions: Put in the capitals and periods.

	a boy took his mom to the movies he had a good time the movie was very funny his mom bought a big box of popcorn they rode home on their bikes

Part C

Instructions: Fix up the run-on sentences in this passage.

Albert Jackson put his finger into a plastic bottle and his finger got stuck in the bottle and he asked his sister to help him. His sister pulled on the bottle. Nothing happened. Albert did not want to go through the rest of his life with a bottle stuck on his finger. Albert was not very happy and his sister got some butter. They rubbed the butter around the top of the bottle. Albert and his sister pulled on the bottle once more. Nothing happened. The bottle didn't come off and Albert got very mad. He hit the table with both hands as hard as he could. The bottle came off. Albert was once more a happy boy.

Part D

Instructions: Write a paragraph that reports on what happened. Write sentences that tell the main thing each numbered person or thing did.

threw	dove	looked	crawled	carried	tried
under	house	catch	patted	their	

Check 1: Does each sentence begin with a capital and end with a period?

Check 2: Does each sentence tell what a person or thing did, not what a person or thing was doing?

Check 3: Does each sentence report on the main thing a person or thing did in the picture?

Lesson 36

Part A

Instructions: Fix up the run-on sentences in this passage.

A girl wanted to buy her brother a birthday present and a friend told her that the girl's brother wanted a puppy. The girl asked her parents if it would be all right to get a puppy. Her parents told her that it was all right. The girl bought a puppy and her dad built a dog house for the puppy. Her brother woke up early on his birthday. The dog was sitting in his room and the boy thanked his sister for the great present.

Part B

1. Serena opened the door and looked in to the room.

2. Anita stood up and stretched her arms.

3. His uncle bent down and looked at the tire.

Part C

Instructions: Edit the passage for these checks:

Check 1: Does any sentence begin with *and?*
Check 2: Does each word that is part of a person's name begin with a capital letter?

Helen and jerome were exploring a cave. And the cave was very dark and very big. It was filled with bats and mice. Helen tripped over something. And she looked up and saw a chest full of gold coins. The children dragged the chest out of the cave. And they brought it to their home. Their dad called Mrs. adams. She knew all about gold coins. And Mrs. adams told helen and jerome that the coins were really gold. The children were so happy that they did three somersaults, two cartwheels and eight backward flips.

Part D

Instructions: Write a paragraph that reports on what happened.

threw	hornets' nest	rock	fell	branch	ground
pond	chased		flew		jumped

Check 1: Does each sentence begin with a capital and end with a period?

Check 2: Does each sentence tell what the person or thing did, not what the person or thing was doing?

Check 3: Does each sentence report on what the person or thing did in the picture?

Lesson 37

Part A

1. The boy ran down the sidewalk and he did not want to be late for school.

2. The boy got up and sat on his bed.

3. The girl ran back into the room and she looked for her coat and she had left her keys in her coat pocket.

4. Michael loved to bake cakes and he baked twenty-five cakes yesterday.

5. Ramon stood up and walked to the door.

Part B

Part C

Instructions: Put in the capitals and periods.

	a girl threw a ball to her brother she threw the ball too hard it rolled into the street the boy started to run into the street a truck moved toward the boy a woman saw the truck she grabbed the boy the truck ran over the ball the woman told the boy to be more careful

Part D

Instructions: Copy the good title sentence. Then write a paragraph that reports on what happened.

> The zookeeper made a trail of bananas.
> The zookeeper tricked the hungry gorilla.
> The gorilla ate the bananas.

| gorilla | walked | bananas | trail | picked |
| closed | escaped | followed | people | |

Check 1: Are there any run-on sentences in your paragraph?

Check 2: Does each sentence begin with a capital and end with a period?

Check 3: Does each sentence tell what the person or thing did, not what the person or thing was doing?

Check 4: Did you tell all the important things that must have happened?

Lesson 37   113

Part A

Instructions: Put in the capitals and periods.

	a little boy left his bike in the street a truck ran over the bike the truck wrecked the bike the truck driver spent all night fixing the bike it looked as good as new in the morning

Part B

Instructions: Fix up the run-on sentences in this passage.

Dennis always carried an umbrella to school and everybody asked him why he carried the umbrella. He told his friends that if it rained he would be ready. Rain started to fall one day after school. Dennis opened his umbrella and it had a big hole in it. The water ran all over Dennis. Dennis does not carry an umbrella anymore.

Part C

Part D

1. Rosita stayed up late and she read a book about dinosaurs.

2. Marcus opened the door and walked inside.

3. Barry moved to California and he wrote me two letters and he asked about our baseball team.

4. A girl walked slowly to school and she thought about the big game.

5. His little brother took a deep breath and jumped into the water.

6. Mario read a book about the stars and he liked to watch the stars at night.

Part E

Instructions: Write a paragraph that reports on what happened.

balloon	bought	tripped	rock	string	floated
air	caught	brought	its beak		

Check 1: Are there any run-ons in your paragraph?

Check 2: Does each sentence begin with a capital and end with a period?

Check 3: Does each sentence tell what the person or thing did, not what the person or thing was doing?

Check 4: Did you tell all the important things that must have happened?

Lesson 39

Part A

Instructions: Fix up the run-on sentences.

1. Tom heard a loud noise and he ran outside and he saw a big cow standing in the grass.

2. The man picked up the ball and threw it back to the children.

3. Lacole was very excited and she knew that today was the last day of school.

4. Rosa held her breath and jumped into the pool.

5. Jill had two dogs and she liked to play with the dogs after school.

6. Jamar walked to school in the morning and took the bus home in the afternoon.

Part B

Cherry pie

Part C

Instructions: Put in the capitals and periods.

a girl had a frog it could hop very high the girl brought the frog to school a school bell scared the frog it hopped on the teacher's desk everybody started to laugh the teacher turned around she liked frogs she told the children that they could watch the frog

Part D

Instructions: Write a paragraph that reports on what happened.

barrel	rolled	truck	crashed	hill
an apple	tree	teacher	boy	caught

Check 1: Are there any run-ons in your paragraph?

Check 2: Does each sentence begin with a capital, end with a period and tell what happened?

Check 3: Did you tell all the important things that must have happened?

Test 3

Part A

Instructions: Fix up the run-on sentences in this passage.

A boy threw a Frisbee to his dog and the Frisbee landed behind a bush. The boy heard a noise coming from behind the bush. He walked around to the other side of the bush. He saw a small animal playing with the Frisbee and the animal had a big white stripe and the animal did not look happy. The animal was a skunk. It was very angry. It made a big stink and the boy ran away from the skunk as fast as he could run.

Part B

Instructions: Cross out some of the names and write *he, she* or *they.*

My brother and my sister stayed home last night. My brother and my sister had lots of homework. My brother worked on math for two hours. My brother had four pages of problems to work. My sister studied for her spelling test. My sister had fifty words to learn.

Part C

Instructions: Put in the capitals and periods.

	Kevin and Michael saw a
	bird on the ground the poor
	bird had crashed into a tree
	it looked very weak the boys
	took the bird home their
	mom knew a great deal about
	taking care of animals she
	made a little nest for the
	bird their mom spent hours
	taking care of the little bird
	the bird got stronger and
	stronger each day

Part D

Instructions: Write a paragraph that reports on what happened.

Frisbee	bushes	bark	climb	appeared
growl	heard	caught	threw	field

Check 1: Are there any run-on sentences in your paragraph?

Check 2: Does each sentence begin with a capital and end with a period?

Check 3: Does each sentence tell what the person or thing did, not what the person or thing was doing?

Check 4: Did you tell all the important things that happened?

Lesson 41

Part A

Instructions: Fix up the run-on sentences in this passage.

A boy threw a stick at a tree and the stick missed the tree. The stick went into a bush. The boy walked toward the bush. He wanted to get the stick. The bush started to shake and the boy stopped walking and a funny looking animal walked out from behind the bush. The animal had a big white stripe down its back. The animal was a skunk. It was mad. The stick had hit the skunk. The skunk made a terrible smell and the boy spent hours in the bathtub that night. The boy never forgot that day.

Part B

Instructions: Fix up the passage so that each sentence begins with a capital and ends with a period.

	a man took a big egg out of a nest. The man brought the egg to his house he thought that the egg might be worth a lot of money. The doorbell rang the man walked to the door. He opened the door a big bird flew into the room. It picked up the egg the man fainted. The big bird flew away with the egg

Part C

1. Tom lived on a farm and he was nine years old.

2. Tyrell put on his new coat and ran outside.

3. Roberto could not find his dog and he looked all over for the dog and he was very worried.

4. Jane ate two eggs and drank a glass of orange juice.

5. Mrs. Lee stood up and clapped her hands.

6. Mrs. Lopez walked to work and she worked downtown.

Part D

Instructions: Write a paragraph that reports on what happened.

cowboy	horse	jumped	snake	crawled	tried
	galloped	away	waved	called	

Check 1: Are there any run-ons in your paragraph?

Check 2: Does each sentence begin with a capital and end with a period?

Check 3: Did you tell all the important things that must have happened?

Lesson 41   **125**

Lesson 42

Part A

Instructions: Fix up the run-on sentences in this passage.

Tom made some cookies and he put them in a shoe box and he put the shoe box in a corner of the kitchen. He went outside to play. Susan started cleaning the kitchen and she did not know what was in the shoe box and she threw the shoe box away. Tom got hungry. He went into the kitchen. He looked for the shoe box. It was gone. He asked Susan if she had seen the shoe box and she told him she had thrown it away. Tom told Susan what was in the shoe box. Susan helped Tom make another batch of cookies.

Part B

Instructions: Use *was* or *were* to complete each sentence.

1. The boy and the girl _____ scared.

2. The little dog _____ hungry.

3. The boys _____ tired.

4. A dog and a cat _____ chasing the birds.

5. The game _____ almost over.

6. The dishes _____ dirty.

7. Ramon and Tammy _____ not at home.

Part C

Instructions: Fix up the passage so that each sentence begins with a capital and ends with a period.

	a spaceship landed near the school. a spaceman walked out of the spaceship he had four arms and six legs. He walked over to the ball closet. he took out seven rubber balls. He started to juggle the balls. the children clapped the school bell rang. the spaceman ran back to his ship it took off. the teachers wondered why the children were so noisy when they came in from recess.

Part D

Instructions: Write a paragraph that reports on what happened.

candle	shelf	pile of newspapers	jumped
fell	woman	bucket	poured	fire
	picked up	knocked	burn	

Check 1: Are there any run-ons in your paragraph?

Check 2: Does each sentence begin with a capital and end with a period?

Check 3: Did you tell all the important things that must have happened?

Lesson 43

Part A

Instructions: Edit the passage for these checks:

Check 1: Are there any run-on sentences?
Check 2: Does each sentence tell what happened?

Sam went hiking in the woods with his dog. Sam didn't watch the ground carefully and he trip over a log and hurt his leg. Sam's dog ran through the woods to get help. The dog saw some people having a picnic and the dog took the people's lunch basket and it ran away with the lunch basket in its mouth. The people chase the dog. The dog ran back to Sam. The people saw Sam lying on the ground and they carried him to their car and a woman drove the car to the hospital. Sam thank the people for helping him. A doctor fix Sam's leg and Sam bought a big bone for his smart dog when they got home.

Part B

Instructions: Use *was* or *were* to complete each sentence.

1. Juan and Jason _____ eating lunch.

2. The boy _____ sleeping.

3. The boys _____ walking home.

4. Tonya and Elisha _____ sick.

5. My little sister _____ not at school.

6. The girl and the boy _____ happy.

7. The cats _____ hungry.

8. The little boy _____ scared.

Part C

Part D

Instructions: Fix up the passage so that each sentence begins with a capital and ends with a period.

	ellen got a bike for her
	birthday. it was too big for her.
	jane got a bike on her birthday
	it was too small for her. the
	girls traded bikes they now
	have bikes that are the right
	size.

Part E

Instructions: Write a paragraph that reports on what happened.

tried	fly	fly swatter	flew	landed
window		cherries	baker	missed
wiped	face	splattered	apron	cleaned

Check 1: Are there any run-ons in your paragraph?

Check 2: Does each sentence begin with a capital and end with a period?

Check 3: Did you tell all the important things that must have happened?

Lesson 43   **131**

Part A

Instructions: Edit the passage for these checks:

Check 1: Are there any run-on sentences?
Check 2: Does each sentence tell what happened?

Marcos was happy when the school bell rang and he want to get home quickly and he had forgotten to clean the kitchen after the birthday party last night. Marcos ran home from school. He took a deep breath and open the door. He couldn't believe his eyes and the room was filthy and Marcos knew he had made a mistake. His mom had told him to clean the kitchen before leaving for school. Marcos ran to the closet and got a broom. He swept the floor and wash the walls. He finish cleaning at 5 o'clock and his mom walk in ten minutes later and Marcos told her what happen. She look at the clean room. She smile and thanked him for doing such a good job.

Part B

Part C

Instructions: Edit the passage for these checks:

Check 1: Do any sentences begin with *and* or *and then?*
Check 2: Do all the words that are part of a person's name begin with a capital?

tonya jackson was playing baseball. And her team was losing two to one. tonya was at bat. The pitcher threw the ball to tonya. tonya swung. She missed the ball. And tonya was mad. The pitcher threw the ball toward Tonya again. And then Tonya swung. She hit the ball. And it went far over everybody's head. Tonya ran around the bases. Her team won the game. And then all the girls clapped for tonya.

Part D

Instructions: Use *was* or *were* to complete each sentence.

1. A boy and a girl _____ standing near the lake.

2. Five birds _____ sitting on a wire.

3. My sister _____ happy.

4. The man and his dog _____ tired.

5. Brittany _____ not scared of snakes.

6. A fork and a spoon _____ lying on the floor.

Part E

Instructions: Copy the title sentence. Then write a paragraph that tells what happened. Tell what the people or things did, but don't tell what people said.

A woman saved a boy.

bounced	over	toward	street	brakes	tried
picked		grabbed	rolled	truck	

Check 1: Are there any run-on sentences in your paragraph?

Check 2: Does each sentence begin with a capital, end with a period and tell what happened?

Check 3: Did you tell all the important things that must have happened?

Lesson 45

Part A

Instructions: Edit the passage for these checks:

Check 1: Are there any run-on sentences?
Check 2: Does each sentence tell what happened?

Ann want to make a big meal for her dad and it was his birthday today. Ann ran home after school and went straight to the kitchen. Ann start to cook and she cook a big meatloaf and she put the meatloaf in the refrigerator. She made a milkshake for herself. Her brother walk into the kitchen and he was carrying a big meatloaf and he had made the meatloaf at a neighbor's house. The children heard a noise at the door. Their mother walk into the room. She also had a meatloaf and they all start to laugh. The family had meatloaf for dinner. Everybody had meatloaf sandwiches for the rest of the week.

Part B

Instructions: Use *was* or *were* to complete each sentence.

1. The dog and the cat _____ sleeping.

2. Six girls _____ running up the hill.

3. A little frog _____ making a big noise.

4. Jason and his sister _____ hungry.

5. My older brother _____ sick yesterday.

6. Her friends _____ not home.

Part C

 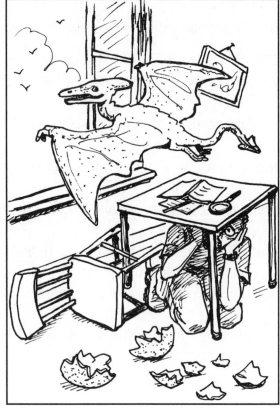

Part D

A boy walked outside. The day was very warm. So the boy took off his shirt. The boy ran five miles. So he got very sweaty. The sun went down. And so the air got colder. The boy did not put his shirt on. So he woke up the next morning with a bad cold.

Part E

Instructions: Copy the title sentence. Then write a paragraph that tells what happened. Tell what the people or things did, but don't tell what people said.

A whale helped a girl.

girl	whale	boat	crashed	boards	tied
tail	shore	toward	water	held	rope
	pulled	pieces	attached		

Check 1: Are there any run-on sentences in your paragraph?

Check 2: Does each sentence begin with a capital, end with a period and tell what happened?

Check 3: Did you tell all the important things that must have happened?

Lesson 46

Part A

Instructions: Edit the passage for these checks:

Check 1: Are there any run-on sentences?
Check 2: Does each sentence tell what happened?

A tiger watch the children playing in the jungle and the tiger was not hungry and it was lonely. A boy saw the tiger and scream. The children start to run away and the tiger began to cry when the children ran away. The children stopped running and a little girl felt sorry for the tiger and she walk up to the tiger and gave it a big hug. The other children watch and the tiger start to lick the little girl's face. The tiger had new friends. It was never lonely again.

Part B

Part C

Instructions: Cross out *was* and write *were* if a sentence names more than one person or thing.

Michael and Angela was getting ready for a spelling test. They had 45 spelling words to learn by Friday. The words was not very hard. Michael tested Angela first. She was not sure how to spell three words. Angela tested Michael next. He was not sure how to spell one word. They studied the words they missed. They was looking forward to the test. They were sure they would do very well.

Part D

The children's dad went to the store. And then he bought three apples. And then he gave one apple to his son and one apple to his daughter. And then the children made an apple pie. And they gave a big piece of the apple pie to their dad.

Part E

Instructions: Copy the title sentence. Then write a paragraph that tells what happened. Tell what the people or things did, but don't tell what people said.

A man found a huge egg.

found	egg	forest	man	picked	hatched
reptile	flew	broke	hid	table	wrecked
	chair	picture	window		

Check 1: Are there any run-on sentences in your paragraph?

Check 2: Does each sentence begin with a capital, end with a period and tell what happened?

Check 3: Did you tell all the important things that must have happened?

Lesson 47

Part A

Instructions: Fix up the passage so that each sentence begins with a capital and ends with a period.

	a man saw a butterfly it had purple and white spots. The man wanted to catch the butterfly he got a net. He started to chase the butterfly it flew over a pond. The man fell into the pond. the pretty butterfly flew away

Part B

Part C

Instructions: Edit the passage for these checks:

Check 1: Did the writer begin any sentences with *so?*
Check 2: Did the writer use the word *was* when a sentence named more than one thing?

Carlos and Vanessa were looking for their dogs. The dogs was not in the house. So the house was empty. So Vanessa pointed to the garden. The dogs was playing in the garden. The children looked at the dogs. The dogs was covered with dirt. So Carlos and Vanessa spent that evening giving the dogs a bath. So Carlos and Vanessa put a fence around the garden the next day.

Part D

Instructions: Copy the title sentence. Then write a paragraph that tells what happened. Tell what the people or things did, but don't tell what people said.

An elephant helped a man.

circus truck	elephant trainer	ramp	spare tire
wheel	tusks	bolts	loosened

Check 1: Are there any run-on sentences in your paragraph?

Check 2: Does each sentence begin with a capital, end with a period and tell what happened?

Check 3: Did you tell all the important things that must have happened?

Part A

Instructions: Edit the passage for these checks:

Check 1: Are there any run-on sentences?
Check 2: Does each sentence tell what happened?

A man went fishing at the lake and he row his boat out into the middle of the lake and he thought about eating fish that night for dinner. A fish saw the man's fishing line. The fish did not want to be eaten and it decided to fool the fisherman and it hook an old shoe on the end of the fishing line. The fisherman pull the line up and he thought that a fish was on the line and he was angry when he saw the old shoe. The fisherman threw his line back into the water and the fish fool him again. It hook an old tire on the fisherman's line. The fisherman pull up the line and he was very angry when he saw the tire. The fisherman row back to shore and went home.

Part B

Instructions: Use *was* or *were* to complete each sentence.

1. The birds _____ flying above the clouds.

2. Maria and her sister _____ sleeping.

3. His little brother _____ sick.

4. The keys _____ under the coat.

5. The dog and the cat _____ playing.

6. My new toy _____ broken.

Part C

Instructions: Edit the passage for these checks:

Check 1: Do any sentences begin with *and* or *and then*?
Check 2: Does each word that is a person's name begin with a capital?

Ellen and her brother wanted to build a bench. They bought a book about building benches. And then ellen bought some wood. And then her brother sawed the wood into small pieces. They nailed the pieces together very carefully. And ellen made sure that no nails were sticking out of the wood. And they painted the bench red, white and blue.

Part D

Instructions: Copy the title sentence. Then write a paragraph that tells what happened. Tell what the person or things did, but don't tell what the person said.

Mr. Wingate had a bad day.

| climb | growl | against | butterfly | chase | bear |

Check 1: Are there any run-on sentences in your paragraph?
Check 2: Does each sentence begin with a capital, end with a period and tell what happened?
Check 3: Did you tell all the important things that must have happened?

Lesson 48 **145**

Lesson 49

Part A

Instructions: Edit the passage for these checks:

Check 1: Are there any run-on sentences?
Check 2: Does each sentence tell what happened?

Alice want to give her dog a bath and she fill the bathtub with warm water and she went outside to look for the dog. The dog hid under the porch. Alice knew where the dog liked to hide. She walk to the porch and pick up the dog. Alice carried the dog to the bathroom and she put the dog into the warm water and she rubbed soap into the dog's fur with a brush. The dog tried to get out of the tub and it jump up and down and it splash water all over Alice. Alice wash and wash. She didn't stop until the dog was clean.

Part B

Instructions: Use *was* or *were* to complete each sentence.

1. A pen and a pencil _____ missing.

2. Her shoes _____ wet.

3. A big dog _____ sitting on the car.

4. LaToya and her brother _____ playing on the sidewalk.

5. The boys _____ not tired.

6. Mrs. Thomas _____ sick yesterday.

Part C

Instructions: Fix up the passage so that each sentence begins with a capital and ends with a period.

	a man went for a walk he
	found a huge egg. He brought
	the egg home the egg started to
	crack. A huge reptile came out
	of the egg it flew around the
	man's house. It knocked over
	chairs and tables it wrecked
	the room. The man opened all
	the windows. The huge reptile
	flew out of the house. The man
	cleaned up the mess.

Part D

Instructions: Copy the title sentence. Then write a paragraph that tells what happened. Tell what the people or things did, but don't tell what people said.

A cowgirl saved a boy.

toward	bull	galloped	trail bike
crashed	charged	fence	horse

Check 1: Are there any run-on sentences in your paragraph?

Check 2: Does each sentence begin with a capital, end with a period and tell what happened?

Check 3: Did you tell all the important things that must have happened?

Test 4

Part A

Instructions: Cross out *was* and write *were* if a sentence names more than one person or thing.

Bill and Sally was getting ready for a spelling test. They had 45 spelling words to learn by Friday. The words was not very hard. Bill tested Sally first. She was not sure how to spell three words. Sally tested Bill next. He was not sure how to spell one word. They studied the words they missed. They was looking forward to the test. They were sure that they would do very well.

Part B

Instructions: Fix up the run-on sentences in this passage.

Ann wanted to make a big meal for her dad and it was his birthday today. Ann ran home after school and went straight to the kitchen. Ann started to cook and she made a big meatloaf and put it in the refrigerator. She went upstairs and waited for her dad. Her brother walked into the kitchen and he was very hungry and he ate the whole meatloaf. Ann could not believe her eyes when she came back to the kitchen. She told her brother why she had cooked the meatloaf. Her brother was a nice guy. He took the whole family to a restaurant and everybody ordered meatloaf.

Part C

Instructions: Fix up the passage so each sentence tells what happened.

A boy threw a ball at a tree. The ball miss the tree and go into a bush. The boy walk toward the bush to get the ball. The bush start to shake. The boy stopped walking. A funny looking animal walk out from behind the bush and looked at the boy. The animal had a big white stripe down its back. The animal look angry. The boy turn around and began to run. The animal chase after him. The skunk caught up to the boy and made a big stink. The poor boy spent hours in the bathtub that night.

Lesson 50-Test 4   **149**

Part D

Instructions: Copy the title sentence. Then write a paragraph that tells what happened. Tell what the person or things did, but don't tell what the person said.

Tina and her dog had a scary day at the pond.

ice	barricade	icy water	broke
skated	chase	climb	

Check 1: Are there any run-on sentences in your paragraph?

Check 2: Does each sentence begin with a capital, end with a period and tell what happened?

Check 3: Did you tell all the important things that must have happened?

Part A

Instructions: Fix up the passage so that each sentence begins with a capital and ends with a period.

	A girl and a boy looked out the window they couldn't believe their eyes. The ground was covered with snow the children put on their boots and coats. They rushed outside. The boy and girl spent the day playing in the snow they built a huge snowman. Their mom took a picture of the snowman their dad put one of his hats on the snowman's head.

Part B

Instructions: Edit the passage for these checks:

Check 1: Are there any run-on sentences?
Check 2: Does each sentence tell what happened?

Mr. Adams want to paint his house and he let Jill and Larry help him. Jill took a bucket of brown paint. She paint the back of the house. Larry took a bucket of green paint. He paint the front of the house. Mr. Adams came out to look at his house and he saw that his house was paint in two colors and he told Jill and Larry to paint the house again. Larry took the brown paint. He paint over the green part of the house. Jill took the green paint. She paint over the brown part of the house. Mr. Adams look at his house again and it was still brown and green and Mr. Adams decided he like his house with two colors and he did not ask Jill and Larry to paint the house again. Mr. Adams had the only house in town paint two different colors.

Part C

Instructions: Copy the title sentence. Then write a paragraph that tells what happened. Tell what the people or things did, but don't tell what people said.

The boys had a bad day.

1.	2.	3.

| skunk   pond   terrible   their clothes   shore   ground |
| laughed   noses   boys' clothes |

Check 1: Are there any run-on sentences in your paragraph?
Check 2: Does each sentence begin with a capital, end with a period and tell what happened?
Check 3: Did you tell all the important things that must have happened?

Part A

Instructions: Fix up the passage so that each sentence begins with a capital and ends with a period.

	Luis and Yoko went skating
	they skated all day. Yoko could
	skate very well she had learned
	to skate at school. Luis had
	never been skating he did not
	know anything about skating.
	Yoko helped Luis. She showed
	him how to keep from falling
	down Luis fell down only two
	times.

Part B

Instructions: Use *was* or *were* to complete each sentence.

1. The cats _____ sleeping under the house.

2. The keys _____ in her pocket.

3. His younger brother _____ taller than their mother.

4. Ramon and his younger brother _____ both taller than their mother.

5. Her best friend _____ not in school today.

6. A little cat and a big dog _____ friends.

Part C

Instructions: Copy the title sentence. Then write a paragraph that tells what happened. Tell what the people or things did, but don't tell what they said.

A girl prevented an accident.

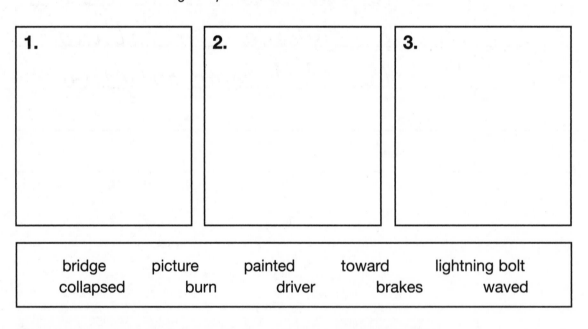

| 1. | 2. | 3. |

| bridge | picture | painted | toward | lightning bolt |
| collapsed | burn | driver | brakes | waved |

Check 1: Are there any run-on sentences in your paragraph?
Check 2: Does each sentence begin with a capital, end with a period and tell what happened?
Check 3: Did you tell all the important things that must have happened?

Lesson 53

Part A

Instructions: Edit the passage for these checks:

Check 1: Are there any run-on sentences?
Check 2: Does each sentence tell what happened?

A girl and her father walk past an old house and they saw smoke coming from the back of the house and the house was on fire. Her dad called the fire department and the girl heard a noise coming from the house. She look up and saw two kittens on the roof. The girl's father point to a ladder lying on the ground and it was big enough to reach the roof. The girl and her father lean the ladder against the side of the house. Her dad climb the ladder and the kittens were standing near the roof's edge. The girl's dad grabbed the kittens and climb down the ladder.

Part B

Instructions: Edit the passage for these checks:

Check 1: Does each sentence begin with a capital and end with a period?

Check 2: Did the writer use the word *were* when a sentence named more than one person?

	The people waited for the bus they was not very happy. The bus was 15 minutes late a big store was near the bus stop the store sold skates. Two women was working in the store they saw the angry people. They carried out a pile of skates to the bus stop. The people was now even angrier because the bus still had not arrived. The women sold the skates to the people The people skated home.

Part C

Instructions: Copy the title sentence. Then write a paragraph that tells what happened. Tell what the people or things did, but don't tell what people said.

The boy had a lucky day.

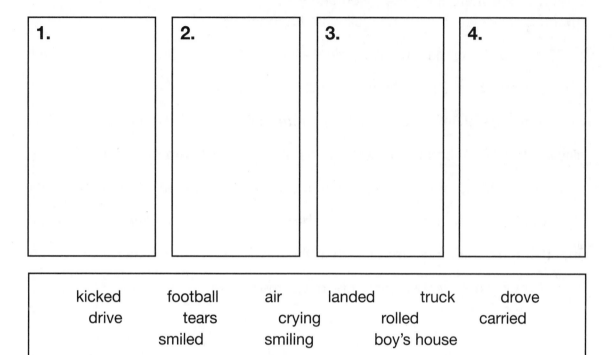

1.	2.	3.	4.

kicked	football	air	landed	truck	drove
drive	tears	crying	rolled		carried
smiled		smiling	boy's house		

Check 1: Are there any run-on sentences in your paragraph?

Check 2: Does each sentence begin with a capital, end with a period and tell what happened?

Check 3: Did you tell all the important things that must have happened?

Lesson 54

Part A

Instructions: Edit the passage for these checks:

Check 1: Are there any run-on sentences?
Check 2: Does each sentence tell what happened?

Tina and Betty had a pillow fight and Tina threw the pillows from her bed at Betty and Betty threw the pillows from her bed at Tina. The girls went into the living room to find more pillows and Betty took all the pillows from the couch. Tina took all the pillows from the chairs. Betty and Tina start to fight again. They threw the pillows at each other until their mother came downstairs and she ask the girls to play more quietly and the girls told their mother that they were sorry for making so much noise. They went upstairs and clean up their room.

Part B

Instructions: Fix up the passage so that each sentence begins with a capital and ends with a period.

A boy wanted to go to the movies. A new space monster movie was playing at the movie theater. The boy did not have any money he asked his mom what he could do to earn some money she told him he could clean the kitchen. The boy cleaned the kitchen his mom gave him money for the movies. His mom also liked space monster movies The boy and his mom went to the movies that night.

Lesson 54   159

Part C

Instructions: Copy the title sentence. Then write a paragraph that tells what happened. Tell what the people or things did, but don't tell what people said.

The dog had a bad day.

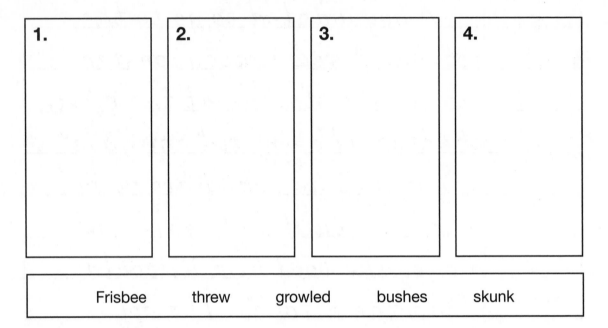

| 1. | 2. | 3. | 4. |

| Frisbee | threw | growled | bushes | skunk |

Check 1: Are there any run-on sentences in your paragraph?

Check 2: Does each sentence begin with a capital, end with a period and tell what happened?

Check 3: Did you tell all the important things that must have happened?

End-of-Program Test

Part A

Instructions: Fix up the run-on sentences.

1. Tom heard a loud noise and he ran outside and he saw a big cow standing in the grass.

2. The man picked up the ball and threw it back to the children.

3. Kim was very excited and she knew that today was the last day of school.

4. Ann held her breath and jumped into the pool.

5. Vanessa had two dogs and she liked to play with the dogs after school.

6. James walked to school in the morning and took the bus home in the afternoon.

Part B

Instructions: Edit the passage for these checks:

Check 1: Are there any run-on sentences?
Check 2: Does each sentence tell what happened?

Ann wanted to make a big cake for her mom and it was her birthday today. Ann ran home after school and went straight to the kitchen. Ann started to bake and she baked a big cake and she put the cake into the refrigerator. Then she made a milkshake for herself. Her brother walked into the kitchen and he was carrying a big cake and he had made the cake at a neighbor's house. The children heard a noise at the door. Their father walked into the room. He also had a cake and they all started to laugh. The family had cake for dessert. Everybody had cake for the rest of the week.

Part C

Instructions: Put in the missing capitals and periods.

a man took a big egg out of a nest. The man brought the egg to his house he thought that the egg might be worth a lot of money. The door bell rang the man walked to the door. He opened the door a big bird flew into the room. It picked up the egg the man fainted. The big bird flew away with the egg

Part D

Instructions: Copy the title sentence. Then write a paragraph that tells what happened. Tell what the people or things did, but don't tell what the person said.

Mr. Wingate had a bad day.

| | climb | growl | against | bush |
| missed | | butterfly | chase | bear's head |

Check 1: Are there any run-on sentences in your paragraph?

Check 2: Does each sentence begin with a capital, end with a period and tell what happened?

Check 3: Did you tell all the important things that must have happened?